AUTOMOBILES

TRAVELING MACHINES

Jason Cooper

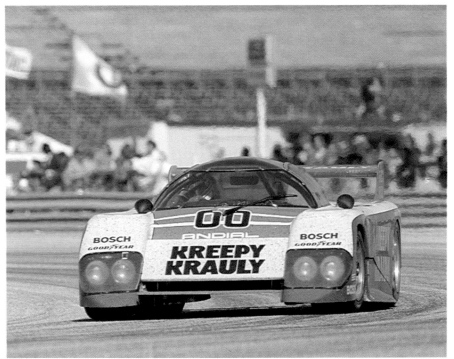

Rourke Enterprises, Inc.
Vero Beach, Florida 32964

PHOTO CREDITS

© Lynn M. Stone: pages 4, 7, 8, 10, 17, and cover;
© Winston Luzier/Lightwave Photography: pages 12, 18, and
title page; courtesy of Ford Motor Company, pages 13 and 21;
courtesy of Mercedes-Benz of North America, Inc., page 15

ACKNOWLEDGEMENTS

The author thanks the following for assistance in the preparation
of photos for this book: Bellm's Cars and Music of Yesterday,
Sarasota, Fla.

LIBRARY OF CONGRESS
Library of Congress Cataloging-in-Publication Data
Cooper, Jason, 1942-
   Automobiles / by Jason Cooper.
   p. cm. — (Traveling machines)
   Includes index.
   Summary: Examines the history of automobiles and surveys
the different types.
   ISBN 0-86592-495-3
   1. Automobiles—Juvenile literature. [1. Automobiles.]
I. Title. II. Series: Cooper, Jason, 1942-   Traveling machines.
TL147.C63 1991
629.222—dc20   90-28334
                    CIP
Printed in the USA   AC

TABLE OF CONTENTS

Automobiles   5

The First Cars   6

Early Cars   9

Modern Cars (1940-1969)   11

Modern Cars (1970-present)   14

Sports Cars   16

Racing Cars   19

Automakers   20

The Wonder of Cars   22

Glossary   23

Index   24

AUTOMOBILES

Automobiles, or cars, come in all sizes, shapes, and colors. There are station wagons, four-door models, **convertibles,** long **limousines,** and sporty, two-door **coupes.**

Whatever their shape, cars have four wheels and a steel frame, or **chassis.** Cars are used to transport people.

The United States has about 130 million automobiles, more than any other nation. The United States also has over 3 million miles of paved roads on which to drive.

Automobiles on interstate highway

THE FIRST CARS

The first cars were built in the late 1800s. They were made by adding engines to open carriages that had once been pulled by horses. The early engines were powered by steam or battery.

Neither steam nor battery power worked well in cars. Gasoline engines, which first appeared in 1895, worked much better. Cars still use gasoline engines.

Henry Ford's Model T Ford (1908) was a major success. In 1913 he began producing it on a moving **assembly line.** Each worker added part of the car as it moved by his or her work station.

1912 Cartercar

EARLY CARS

The assembly line made car-building less expensive and much faster. Automobiles were quickly improved.

Hand cranks for starting engines were replaced by electric starters. Steel roofs replaced soft roofs, and air-filled tires replaced solid tires.

In the 1930s, cars became sleeker in appearance. They also became more powerful.

In 1939, Oldsmobile introduced a car that shifted from one forward **gear** to another by itself.

1930 Ford Model A

MODERN CARS (1940-1969)

During World War II (1939-1945), production of American cars stopped. Automakers built war supplies instead.

When American cars were built again, beginning with 1946 models, they were larger, wider, smoother riding, and lower than earlier cars. By the mid-1950s, cars had become faster and more streamlined.

Many cars were equipped with air-conditioning and power brakes and steering, making them easier to stop and steer. The automatic shift introduced by Oldsmobile in 1939 was being used by all car makers.

1950 Pontiac

1934 Packard, a classic

1964 Ford Mustang convertible

MODERN CARS (1970-present)

Most American cars of the 1960s continued to be big and powerful. In the 1970s, however, there were shortages of oil, from which gasoline is made. Small cars use less gasoline than larger cars, and small cars began to sell rapidly. The small Japanese **imports** did especially well in America.

More and more American cars were made smaller during the 1980s. Fuel economy and safety bcame more important than style and power. By 1990, many cars had built-in air bags to cushion crashes.

1991 Mercedes-Benz 500SL

SPORTS CARS

Sports cars are small and low to the ground. They are not as quiet and comfortable as big cars, but they are fast, beautiful, and built to hug the road.

One of the first sports cars was a 1914 Stutz Bearcat. Like many modern sports cars, the Bearcat was a convertible and sat just two people.

Many of the sports cars on North American highways are imports. A popular American sports car is Chevrolet's Corvette.

1986 Chevrolet Corvette convertible

RACING CARS

Stock car races match cars that are much like the vehicles people buy from an auto dealer. Stock cars often race on dirt tracks at speeds of 100 miles per hour and greater.

Formula One, or Grand Prix, cars are one-seat cars built just for racing. These little cars with their huge tires can travel over 200 miles per hour.

Indy cars, the racing cars used at the famous Indianapolis 500 Race, are similar to Formula One cars.

Chevrolet Lumina stock car racing

AUTOMAKERS

Automakers are the companies that design and produce automobiles. Early in American auto history, about 2,000 companies made cars. By 1920, the number of American automakers had shrunk to 100. Today there are just three—Ford, Chrysler, and General Motors, the largest. Each company makes several cars. Some of the General Motors vehicles, for example, are Chevrolet, Oldsmobile, and Cadillac.

About 8 million American cars are produced each year by the three companies. The world's largest producer of automobiles is Japan.

Ford Motor Company assembly line, 1913

THE WONDER OF CARS

North Americans love the wonder of a shiny, new automobile. North Americans also love **classic** cars. A few car models, especially those built between 1925 and 1948, are classics. These are the finest cars of their time. Each was made in small numbers. They were costly when they were new, and they are worth even more now.

Among the classics are certain Packards, Lincolns, Cadillacs, Cords, Auburns, Mercedes-Benzes, and others.

The automobile—a wonder of speed, power, comfort, and design.

Glossary

assembly line (uh SEM blee LINE) — a process in which a product is put together as it passes from one worker to the next

chassis (CHA see) — the frame and many of the important, working parts of a vehicle

classic (KLA sick) — something of proven excellence and value, such as certain older cars

convertible (kun VER tih bull) — an auto with a top that can be lowered or removed

coupe (KOOP) — a closed, two-door automobile

gear (GEER) — a position in a car's power system that changes the car's power or direction

import (IM port) — something that is brought into a country from a foreign country

limousine (LIHM eh zeen) — a large, comfortable car that is specially built to be extra long

stock car (STAHK KAR) — an automobile that is raced, but that is similar to cars kept in dealers' stock for sale to anyone; a "regular" car used for racing

INDEX

air-conditioning   11
Auburn   22
automakers   11, 20
Cadillac   20, 22
cars
    classic   22
    early   6, 9
    Formula One   19
    Grand Prix   19
    Indy   19
    modern   11, 14
    number of   5, 20
    racing   19
    safety of   14
    shapes of   5
    size of   11, 14
    speed of   11, 16, 19
    sports   16
    stock   19
    style of   9, 11, 16
chassis   5
Chevrolet   16, 20
Chrysler   20
convertible   5, 16
Cord   22
Corvette   16

coupe   5
engines   6
Ford, Henry   6
Ford, Model T   6
Ford Motor Company   20
gasoline   6, 14
gear   9
General Motors   20
hand crank   9
imports   14, 16
Indianapolis 500 Race   19
Japan   20
limousine   5
Lincoln   22
Mercedes-Benz   22
Oldsmobile   9, 11, 20
Packard   22
power brakes   11
power steering   11
roads   5
roof   9
starter, electric   9
station wagon   5
Stutz Bearcat   16
tires   9, 19
World War II   11